Take Command of Your Self-Esteem

Debbie Bills

chipmunkapublishing

the mental health publisher

All rights reserved, no part of this publication may be reproduced by any means, electronic, mechanical photocopying, documentary, film or in any other format without prior written permission of the publisher.

Published by

Chipmunkapublishing

PO Box 6872

Brentwood

Essex CM13 1ZT

United Kingdom

http://www.chipmunkapublishing.com

Copyright © Debbie Bills 2011

Chipmunkapublishing gratefully acknowledge the support of Arts Council England.

Author Biography

Debbie Bills was born in the state of Nebraska USA in 1948.

She grew up on a small farm in the Midwest with a father that was an alcohol and a mother with low self-esteem. After reaching adulthood, she realized some of her choices were due to childhood. With much research and learning she realized why she made many wrong choices and was determined to change her life around. She now understand the draw backs from be raised with an alcoholic father and a mother with low self-esteem.

Her passion is to teach others how to overcome the obstacles that they may face while growing up and be the person they were meant to be.

Debbie Bills

Introduction: Let's Get Started Climbing Confidence Mountain

"The greater the difficulty, the more the glory in surmounting it." Epicurus

What is self-esteem?

self-es·teem
'sɪlf ɪˈstim, ˌsɪlf' [self-**i**-steem, self-] –*noun*

1. A realistic respect for or favourable impression of oneself; self-respect.

The term 'self-esteem' was first used in approximately 1650. It has become the yardstick through which people view themselves. We know that low self-esteem is a bad thing, and high self-esteem is positive. One leads to issues such as anxiety, depression and uncertainty, while the other brings benefits such as confidence, sociability and a lust for life.

The problem with self-esteem is just how difficult it is to define. Definitions for this elusive quality range from valuing the self right through to having the ability to love and be loved. Regardless of where your view on the spectrum of self-esteem lies, there can be no doubt that it is a quality which we all, as human beings, want to own.

Self-esteem makes us more comfortable with ourselves as people. It gives us the clarity of mind to make confident judgements, trusting ourselves to make the right decisions at the right time. It enables us to step out with pride, knowing that we are acting in the right way.

There are more benefits to high self-esteem. People who place value on themselves are more capable, having faith that their actions will bring benefits. They are more sociable, as they know that they have something of value to bring to their family and peer relationships. Above all, people with a good sense of self understand that they are unique, wonderful individuals in their own way. They are quicker to forgive themselves for failings, and more likely to attempt to reach their goals without being held back by doubt and negativity.

All in all, it is self-evident that a good level of pride and self-worth is a massive element of what it means to be human. Without this quality, many people can flounder when it comes to fitting easily and comfortably into their own world. The problem is, self-esteem can be removed much more easily than it can be created. When people go through set-backs which undermine their confidence, or repeatedly undergo experiences such as abuse, negative relationships or parental criticism, they can quickly lose the self-esteem they once had.

The most important place we need to apply esteem is within ourselves. We must maintain our self-esteem, so we place value on ourselves as a worthy individual in the world. Self-esteem affects every single part of our lives. If that esteem is low, we can feel like our life isn't worthy. Elevating esteem for ourselves is the key to happiness in life.

Your own self-esteem is something more fundamental than the normal "ups and downs" associated with situational changes. For people with good basic self-esteem, normal "ups and downs" may lead to temporary fluctuations in the way they feel about themselves, but only to a limited extent. For people with poor self-esteem, these "ups and down" may make all the difference in the world.

People with poor self-esteem rely on how they are doing in the present to determine how they feel about themselves. They need positive external experiences to counteract the negative feelings and thoughts that constantly plague them. The good feeling (from a good grade, etc.) can be only temporary.

Healthy self-esteem is based on our ability to assess ourselves accurately (know ourselves) and still be able to accept and to value ourselves unconditionally. This means being able to realistically acknowledge our strengths and limitations (which is part of being human) and accepting ourselves as worthy and worthwhile without conditions or reservations.

Sometimes we need to raise our self-esteem to levels that will enhance our life and the way we view life. It can make a tremendous difference to our quality of life. Learning techniques to raise self-esteem can be taught and put into practice in just a few days. It does take practice to keep one's self-worth at the forefront.

This book outlines the nature of self-esteem, and demonstrates just how easy it can be to regain a sense of self which is whole, uncritical and forgiving.

The benefits of self-worth bring their own regards, and will help you to be more positive, outgoing, goal-oriented and confident in your day to day life.

Where Does Our Self-Esteem Come From?

"There's a place and means for every man alive."
Shakespeare

Our self-esteem develops and evolves throughout our lives as we build an image of ourselves through our experiences with different people and activities. Experiences during childhood play a particularly large role in the shaping of our basic self-esteem. This can bring about adults who always choose to be happy or unhappy adults.

The idea that self-esteem and self-image are related to how people behave in society, perform in school, react to peer pressure, and interact with others has received a great deal of attention from psychologists and child development experts beginning in the 1980s.There is even a National Association of Self-Esteem (NASE) dedicated to research and teaching on self-esteem issues.

Since the early 1980s, efforts have been made to incorporate activities to raise self-esteem in school curricula and into programmes dealing with young people who have problems with gangs, substance abuse, and the law. Results of these programmes are inconclusive and open to many different interpretations. However, high self-esteem, or liking yourself and feeling confident that you can solve problems, is generally seen as positive. Low self-esteem, or disliking your self-image and feeling you have no choices and cannot influence your life, are generally seen as negative.

When we were growing up, our successes (and failure) and how we were treated by the members of our immediate family, by our teachers, coaches, religious authorities, and by our peers, all contributed to the creation of our basic self-esteem and happiness within.

An adult who has healthy self-esteem was given this gift in childhood. This could have been done in many ways. Probably one of the most important is being praised for accomplishments. Children who are talked to respectfully and listened to also contributed to healthy self-esteem in adulthood. These children were hugged often and given attention and experienced some type of success in school or sporting activities. They grow up into healthy happy adults.

On the other side of the spectrum, we have to identify the childhood for those adults who have poor or low self-esteem. These children were often criticized harshly, were yelled at or beaten, and were given little attention by those they were closet to. They were ridiculed and even teased as they experienced failures in their young lives. They were made to feel they had to be perfect in order to be valued and associated failure in situations as a failure of their whole selves.

Various experts have noted that when parental communication is consistently delivered in a negative style it becomes internalised, and children start to practice negative "self-talk," generating their own self-reinforcing negative messages. Belittling comparisons with siblings ("Why can't you be more like your brother?") and threats of abandonment ("If you don't stop that right now, I'm leaving you here!") are other examples of negative communication from parents that, if used consistently, are thought to lower self-esteem and diminish a child's feelings of love and acceptance.

I am an example of the child that grew up with low self-esteem. My mother had low self-esteem because of her upbringing, and passed it on to her children. I was never beaten, but was always told that I couldn't do anything right. I couldn't clean the house right, wash the dishes right, etc. As a young adult, when I wanted to learn a trade or have a career, I was asked, "Why would anyone want to become that?"

It's sad, isn't it? - To think of a child treated that way. What's even sadder is the effect that kind of treatment has on their lives as adults. We are shaped and moulded by our experiences. Do you recognize yourself?

How we feel about ourselves can influence how we live our lives, whether we choose to be happy and successful or live unhappy lives. People who feel that they are likable and lovable (in other words people with good self-esteem) have better relationships and always choose happiness. They are more likely to ask for help and support from friends and family when they need it. People who believe they can accomplish goals and solve problems are more likely to do well in school. Having good self-esteem allows you to accept yourself and live life to the fullest, being happy within.

Self-esteem plays a role in almost everything we do. People with high self-esteem do better in school and find it easier to make friends. They tend to have better relationships with peers and adults, feel happiness within, find it easier to deal with mistakes, disappointments, and failures, and are more likely to stick with something until they succeed. It takes some work, but it's a skill you'll have for life.

This is a focus on the low self-esteem that many people have these days. You can overcome issues with low self-esteem. It's not as difficult as you might think. In fact, all you have to do is recognize, understand, and use the techniques I shall give you. I have used these techniques on myself to overcome my low self-esteem.

"Instead of comparing our lot with that of those who are more fortunate than we are, we should compare it with the lot of the great majority of our fellow men. It then appears that we are among the privileged."
Helen Keller

What is Self-Esteem?

"Never compare yourself with others, because you are not a replica of anyone." Debbie Bills

Some people think that self-esteem means confidence, and of course confidence comes into it, but it's more than that.

The fact is that there are any number of apparently confident people who can do marvelous things but who have poor self-esteem. Many people in the public eye fall into this category. Actors and comedians and singers in particular can seem to glow with assurance on stage, and yet off stage many of them feel desperately insecure.

Individuals can be stunningly attractive and world famous, and seem poised and perfect, but deep down find it hard to value themselves. Think of the late Princess of Wales and Marilyn Monroe and you'll accept I think that public opinion is no guarantee of self-belief.

If self-esteem isn't quite the same thing as confidence, what is it?

The word 'esteem' comes from a Latin word which means 'to estimate'. Self-esteem is how you estimate yourself.

To do that you need to ask yourself certain questions:

Do I like myself?

Do I think I'm a good human being?

Am I someone deserving of love?

Do I deserve happiness? Do I really feel – both in my mind and deep in my guts, that I'm an OK person?

People with low self-esteem find it hard to answer 'yes' to these questions. Perhaps you are one of them.

Low self esteem results from a poor self image. Your self image is based on how you see yourself. Do you think you are a good, reliable, hard working, honest or friendly person?

Low self esteem also depends on other factors like your job. For example, do you value the job you do? Does the job you have help you be happy with who you are?

Low self esteem feeds your negative thinking and makes you believe negative comments others make. This can cause you to lose confidence, so it is vital to end negative thoughts if you want to build your self esteem.

High self esteem is the opposite of the above! If you have a high level of self esteem you will be confident, happy, highly motivated and have the right attitude to succeed.

Take Command of Your Self-Esteem

Self esteem is crucial and is a cornerstone of a positive attitude towards living.

It is very important because it affects how you think, act and even how you relate to other people. It affects your potential to be successful. Low self esteem means poor confidence, and that also causes negative thoughts which mean that you are likely to give up easily rather than face challenges. In addition, it has a direct bearing on your happiness and well-being.

The concept of self-esteem can be summed up as: Confidence in our ability to think and to cope with the basic challenges of life and confidence in your right to be successful and happy. The feelings of being worthy, deserving, entitled to assert our needs and wants, achieve our values and enjoy the fruits of our efforts.

We also commonly think that self-esteem is merely about how we feel about ourselves at any particular moment. While seemingly existing in degrees, we tend to believe that we have positive or negative self-esteem and that we make that determination simply by how we feel about ourselves.

However, our feelings or emotions do not exist alone or have an independent existence. We do not just simply feel. For every feeling or emotion that we have, either positive or negative, there is a corresponding thought that we have about ourselves that generates the experience of self-esteem.

Whether positive or negative, self-esteem is merely how our mind experiences the thoughts that we have about ourselves. If a person has positive thoughts about himself or herself they will experience positive or good self-esteem. On the other hand, if the individual has negative thoughts about who he or she is then they will experience poor or negative self-esteem.

To truly understand what self-esteem is all about, more importantly to be able to alter it when necessary for one's wellness or healing, we must first get it that we develop or create about ourselves. The thoughts or beliefs that we have about ourselves are crucial in that they determine or create the structure of our experience of self-esteem and the various emotions associated with it.

We also tend to think of our self-esteem as being something that is shaped by the events that take place in our life, particularly those from our past. We tend to believe that who we think we are and how we feel about ourselves is merely the product, effect or caused by the experiences that we have had in the past. It says that we are who we are by virtue of what has happened to us as human beings.

More specifically, we tend to think that the cause in the matter of who we think we are and our self-esteem is due to circumstance, situation or others, people, places and things. We do not tend to think that our self-esteem is something we actually developed or created. Our personal self-esteem is shaped by our past and the experiences we have had in our lives and how we responded to them.

Take Command of Your Self-Esteem

We create our thoughts and with it our emotions from the meaning that we gave to the events that took place in our life, especially at an early age. We give meaning to everything in our life, including and most importantly to ourselves. At an early age the meaning that we give an event is important, but what is especially important is how we made it out to be about our identity.

Say for example at a young age you were taught, "I can do this", when challenged with a new task. You will grow up with a good self-esteem, because you were taught that you could accomplish things. Now on the other hand if you were taught, "You can't do that", you are going to come away with a lower self-esteem.

Living in a state of low self-esteem can be very damaging to the quality of life you lead on a daily basis. Your self-esteem is YOUR opinion of yourself, but far too many people allow others to influence or even make up their opinion for them. It sounds so very silly, but if you think on this you will realize how certain events, comments and encounters helped to "make or break" your self-esteem.

Building esteem is a first step towards your happiness and a better life. If you have low confidence or low self esteem you will find it impossible to be the person you could be and your happiness will be limited.

Self esteem increases your confidence. If you have confidence you will respect yourself and then you can respect others, improve your relationships and become happier. This is not a selfish goal, as you will contribute more and share yourself with the world and those around you.

Low esteem causes depression, unhappiness, insecurity and low confidence. The desires of others may take preference over your own. Inner criticism, that nagging voice of disapproval inside you, causes you to stumble at every challenge, and challenges seem impossible!

Do I Have Low Self-Esteem?

"The greatest difficulty is that men do not think enough of their selves, do not consider what it is that they are sacrificing when they follow in a herd, or when they cater for their establishment." Ralph Emerson

While you might already have a good indication that you are suffering from low self-esteem, it might be a good idea to explore this a little further. The more we explore our personality, the closer we can be to choose happiness with all our choices we make in life.

Take this simple quiz.

Personality Self-Esteem Assessment.

Directions: Answer T if the statement is true for you. Answer F if the statement is false for you.

T F: I am able to discuss my good points, skills, abilities, achievements and successes with others.

T F: I assert myself with someone who I believe is violating or ignoring my rights.

T F: I am content with who I am, how I act, and what I do in life.

T F: I am not bothered by feelings of insecurity or anxiety when I meet people for the first time.

T F: My life is balanced between work, family life, social life, recreation/leisure and spiritual life.

T F: I am aware of the roles I played in my family of origin and have usually been able to make these behavior patterns work for me in my current life.

T F: I am bonded with the significant others in my environment at home, work, school, at play, or in the community

T F: I am able to perform the developmental tasks necessary to ensure my ongoing healthy self-esteem.

T F: I am satisfied with my level of achievement at school, work, home, and in the community.

T F: I am a good problem solver; my thinking is not clouded by irrational beliefs or fears.

T F: I am willing to experience conflict, if necessary to protect my rights.

If you selected F for three or more of the preceding questions, you probably need to work at increasing your self-esteem, so you can find your happiness within. That's what we're here for! But that comes a little later!

There are many, many indicators that a person has low-self-esteem. Consider this list.

People with low self- esteem:

Consider themselves lost, unworthy of being cared for.

Are poor risk takers.

Operate out of a fear of rejection.

Are typically unassertive in their behaviour with others.

Are fearful of conflict with others.

Are hungry for the approval of others.

Are poor problem solvers.

Are distressed with irrational beliefs and have a tendency to think irrationally.

Are susceptible to all kinds of fears.

A tendency to become emotionally stuck and immobilized.

Have a poor "track record" in school or work; conversely, they sometimes over compensate and become over achievers.

Are unable to affirm or to reinforce themselves positively.

Are unable to make an honest assessment of their strengths, qualities, and good points; they find it difficult to accept compliments or recognition from others.

Have poorly defined self-identities with a tendency to just blend in so they can fit in with others.

Are insecure, anxious, and nervous when they are with others.

Often become overcome with anger about their status in life, and are likely to have chronic hostility or chronic depression.

Are easily overcome with despair and depression when they experience a setback or loss in their lives.

Have a tendency to overreact and become de-energized by resentment, anger, and the desire for revenge against those whom they believe have not fully accepted them.

Fulfill roles in their families of origin that are counter-productive and result in disruptive behaviour. These roles carry over into their adult lives.

Are vulnerable to mental health problems and have a tendency to use addictive behaviour to medicate their hurt and pain. Such addictive behavior can include alcohol, drugs, food, gambling, sex, shopping, working too much, or the search for excitement.

Kind of overwhelming, isn't it? Do you recognize yourself in any of these statements? Don't feel alone. Actually, low self-esteem is actually quite a widespread problem. And if you suffer from this problem, it can cause some more, even serious problems.

Low self-esteem can have devastating consequences on happiness within.

It can create anxiety, stress, loneliness and increased likelihood for depression.

It can cause problems with friendships and relationships.

It can seriously impair academic and job performance.

It can lead to underachievement and increase vulnerability to drug and alcohol abuse.

Worst of all, these negative consequences themselves reinforce the negative self-image and can take a person into a downward spiral of lower self-esteem and increasingly non-productive or even actively self-destructive behaviour, which takes away all chances of finding happiness within.

As we go through this do not despair, because we do have to remember that no one is perfect. However, there is always room for improvement and learning about ourselves. Obviously happiness within comes from getting to know our real self and improving what we feel needs to be improved.

Next I shall go into the three different faces that people with low self-esteem wear.

Choose to be happy by knowing that "God doesn't make junk."

3 Faces of Low-Esteem

"God doesn't make junk and don't let anyone tell you otherwise for fear of losing what he has created." Debbie Bills

There are actually three "faces" that people with low self-esteem wear. See if you see yourself in any of these personalities:

The Imposter: acts like they have the secret to happiness and success, but is really terrified of failure. The imposter lives with the constant fear that she or he will be "found out." They need continuous success to maintain the mask of positive self-esteem, which may lead to problems with perfectionism, procrastination, competition and burn-out.

The Rebel: acts like the opinions or good will of others – especially people who are important or powerful - don't matter. The rebel lives with constant anger about not feeling "good enough". They continuously need to prove that others' judgements and criticisms don't hurt, which may lead to problems like blaming others excessively, breaking rules or laws, or fighting authority.

The Loser: acts helpless and unable to cope with the world and waits for someone to come to the rescue. The loser uses self-pity or indifference as a shield against fear of taking responsibility for changing his or her life. They look constantly to others for guidance, which can lead to such problems as lacking assertiveness skills, under-achievement and excessive reliance on others in relationships.

So what does a person with healthy self-esteem look like? These people exhibit happiness within and the following qualities.

Hold themselves as worthy to be loved and to love others, worthy to be cared for and to care for others, worthy to be nurtured and to nurture others, worthy to be touched and supported and to touch and support others, worthy to be listened to and to listen to others, worthy to be recognized and to recognized others, worthy to be encouraged and to encourage others, worthy to be reinforced as "good" people and to recognize others as "good" people. They have chosen happiness.

They are capable of being creative, imaginative problem solvers; of being risk takers, optimistic in their approach to life and in the attainment of their personal goals to keep their happiness within.

Are leaders and are skillful in dealing with people. They are neither too independent nor too dependent on others. They have the ability to size up a relationship and adjust to the demands of the interaction. Have a healthy self-concept. Their perception of themselves is in synchrony with the picture of themselves they project to others.

They are able to accept the responsibility for and consequences of their actions. They do not resort to shifting the blame or using others as scapegoats for actions that have resulted in a negative outcome.

They are altruistic. They have a legitimate concern for the welfare of others. They are not self-centred or egotistical in their outlook on life. They do not take on the responsibility for others in an over-responsible way. They help others accept the responsibility for their own actions. They are, however always ready to help anyone who legitimately needs assistance or guidance.

Have healthy coping skills. They are able to handle the stresses in their lives in a productive way. They are able to put the problems, concerns, issues, and conflicts that come their way into perspective. They are able to keep their lives in perspective without becoming too idealistic or too morose.

They are survivors in the healthiest sense of the word. They have a good sense of humour and are able to keep a balance of work and fun in their lives. In this way they are always choosing happiness.

Look to the future with excitement, a sense of adventure and optimism. They recognize their potential for success and visualize their success in the future. They have dreams, aspirations, and hopes for the future. Nothing is going to take away their happiness within.

They are goal oriented with a sense of balance in working toward their goals. They know from where they have come, where they are now, and where they are going.

Does this sound like someone you want to be like? Well, it can be! There are so many steps you can take to raise your self-worth and stop suffering from low self-esteem. You will be a much better and happier person for it and enjoy a wonderfully fulfilling life of happiness within.

Here is self esteem test written by Karl Perera, author of www.more-selfesteem.com

In this test I would like you to understand were my dreams are for you. This is a test to show you when you have reached good self esteem. This is what we are working toward. Take the test now and after you are through working on your self esteem I would like you to take it again. By doing it this way you are going to see the progress you have made and know what parts need the hardest work.

Just answer TRUE or FALSE to the questions:

1. Other people are not better off or more fortunate than me?
2. I accept myself as I am and am happy with myself?
3. I enjoy socializing?
4. I deserve love and respect?
5. I feel valued and needed?
6. I don't need others to tell me I have done a good job?
7. Being me is important?
8. I make friends easily?

9. I can accept criticism without feeling put down?

10. I admit my mistakes openly?

11. I never hide my true feelings?

12. I always speak up for myself and put my views across?

13. I am a happy, carefree person?

14. I don't worry what others think of my views?

15. I don't need others' approval to feel good?

16. I don't feel guilty about doing or saying what I want?

TEST SCORE: Total number of TRUE answers you gave each one point.

15-16: You have a high level of self esteem.

12-14: Not bad, but room for you to improve.

8-11: Low self esteem is holding you back.

Below 8 points – Your esteem is drastically low.

The Inner Voice

"You were blessed with hands and arms, legs and feet, heart and brains: don't let any of them go to waste by what others may say. You are the flavouring in the cake." Debbie Bills

Our past experiences, even the things we don't usually think about, are all alive and active in our daily life in the form of an inner voice. Although most people do not "hear" this voice in the same way, it is constantly repeating those original messages to us. This can determine our happiness within.

For people with healthy self-esteem the messages of the inner voice are positive and reassuring, which makes for a person to choose happiness. For people with low self-esteem, the inner voice becomes a harsh inner critic, constantly criticizing, punishing, and belittling their accomplishments.

Do you ever find yourself berating yourself for something that you've done? Have you ever found yourself struggling with something that you know you should do but keep talking yourself out of? That's your inner voice. This is going to make for your happiness or unhappiness.

Your inner voice will say things like, "You can't do this". "There's no way you can succeed", and "Why bother trying, you'll just fail". Your inner voice is your harshest critic and the one who will lower your self-esteem the quickest. You need to change that inner voice from a negative influence to a positive one.

We all have an inner voice. You should talk back to it. Combat it. Let it know that you are the one in control, not it! Don't let it take your happiness within away. Let's look at some of the dialogue the inner voice will tell you and healthy ways to rebut what it is saying.

When the inner voice is unfairly harsh.

"People said they liked my presentation, but it was nowhere near as good as it should have been. I can't believe no-one noticed all the places I messed up. I'm such an imposter."

Counteract by being reassuring yourself:

"Wow, they really liked it! Maybe it wasn't perfect, but I worked hard on that presentation and did a good job. I'm proud of myself. This was a great success." With these reactions your happiness within stays intact!

If the inner voice is unrealistically generalizing as in:

"I got an F on the test. I don't understand anything in this class. I'm such an idiot. Who am I fooling? I shouldn't be taking this class. I'm stupid and I don't belong in college."

Tell that inner voice something specific:

"I did poorly on this one test, but I've done OK on all the homework. There are some things here that I don't understand as well as I thought I did, but I can do the material. I've done fine in other classes that were just as tough." With this way you are choosing happiness.

The inner voice might also be extremely illogical:

"He is frowning. He didn't say anything, but I know it means that he doesn't like me!"

Tell that voice something that is purely logical:

"OK, he's frowning, but I don't know why. It could have nothing to do with me. Maybe I should ask."

Finally, the inner voice will take things to extremes:

"She turned me down for a date! I'm so embarrassed and humiliated. No one likes or cares about me. I'll never find a girlfriend. I'll always be alone."

It's time to tell that inner voice things aren't nearly as bad as it makes them out to be.

"Ouch! That hurt. Well, she doesn't want to go out with me. That doesn't mean no one does. I know I'm attractive and a nice person. I'll find someone. I always choose to be happy, so there has to be someone that is going to appreciate that."

In general, when that inner voice begins putting you down, counteract with a positive statement. Don't let that voice overtake you and talk you into something that just isn't true. You are in control, not the inner critic. Take charge and begin the journey toward more positive thinking and your happiness within!

One way to do this is through positive affirmations.

This isn't new age anything, it's simply a way for you to infuse positive self talk into your life and calm that negative inner voice.

Utilizing positive affirmations can be a very powerful tool for transforming what a person thinks about himself and as a result improve the individual's self-esteem. The consistent use of positive affirmations will transform the negative beliefs about who a person thinks he is into positive ones, will begin to alter the basic structure of his self talk or inner voice and produce a transformation from poor self-esteem to positive self-esteem and happiness within. Making you very comfortable in your own skin.

The key to the effective use of positive affirmation or any other type of intervention is consistency. The self-image and the negative thoughts about who a person thinks he or she is that generates his or her experience of poor or negative self-esteem is well established in the their belief system. In many cases the development of a negative self-image took years to create and has been reinforced through repetitive behavioural validation.

Take Command of Your Self-Esteem

Review this list of inspiring words that will help you build your self esteem and feel better about who you are.

Listen to your inner voice and follow it, for it is wisdom and knows what is best for you at all times.

Talk health, happiness and prosperity to everyone that you meet.

Think only of the best, work only for the best and expect only the best. You deserve nothing less.

Care about the happiness and success of others and always offer them help and encouragement.

Forget your past mistakes (they were learning experiences) and focus on your successes while encouraging yourself to greater achievement for the future.

Always do your best and be proud that you gave it your all.

When you help someone, do not ask for anything in return, you will receive your reward.

Positive Affirmations

Positive self-affirmations are healing, positive scripts you give to yourself to counter your negative inner voice. They can help you free yourself from the over-dependence you have on other people's opinions, attitude, or feelings about you and help you feel good about yourself. They will help you find and keep your happiness within.

When you visualize a new order and sense in your life, you can work towards a more positive attitude and take responsibility for your own health and emotional stability. You will let go of negative emotional baggage and be able to deal with your life in a realistic positive manner, which is going to allow you to always choose happiness.

Positive self-affirmations will help you resolve negative feelings from the past so you can face the present with a less obstructed view. In doing this, you will give yourself permission to grow, to change, to take risks, and to create a better life for yourself and your happiness.

You will take a healthy self-oriented route in your life so that you can let go of the people and thoughts that drain your emotional resources and keep you from experiencing full personal health and the happiness within you deserve. When you recognize that you have a right to be a healthy and happy human being, you will have a fighting chance at achieving your full potential.

Success prophecies, when visualized, or believed in, do come true. It's time for you to believe that fully. This is how positive affirmations can affect you and your inner being. The biggest plus is that the negative inner voice will be quieted, allowing you to find the positive inner voice that will help you become a fully happy individual.

There are two areas of self-affirmations we shall work on first. Try using any of these statements the next time you are feeling that negativity come over you.

I am: A statement of who you are

This is a positive affirmation of a real state of being that exists in you. You can achieve a full list of I am statements by taking a personal positive inventory of your attributes, strengths, talents, and competencies. Examples include:

I am competent
I am strong
I am intelligent
I am beautiful
I am a good person
I am caring
I am loving and smart
I am creative and talented
I am energetic and enthusiastic
I am relaxed, joyful and trusting
I am generous, courageous and forgiving
I am open, happy and sharing.

I can: A statement of your potential

This is a positive affirmation of your ability to accomplish goals. It is a statement of your belief in your power to grow, to change, and to help yourself. Examples include:

I can lose weight
I can stop smoking
I can handle my children
I can gain self-confidence
I can take risks
I can be a winner
I can be strong
I can pass calculus
I can laugh and have fun
I can be assertive
I can control my temper
I can grow as a person
I can heal
I can let go of guilt
I can let go of fear
I can change
I can be positive
I can be a problem solver
I can handle my own problems
I can be honest with my feelings
I can let go of being compulsive
I can succeed

Words of inspiration are something that we can always use on that rainy day:

I Know You Can!

Positive Change in Your Life

"Look not mournfully into the past, it comes not back again. Wisely improve the present, it is thine. Go forth to meet the shadowy future without fear and with a manly heart." Henry Wadsworth Longfellow

I do: A statement of positive change in your life

This is a positive affirmation of a change you want to achieve. It is a positive statement of what you want to happen. It is a success prophecy for your secret to happiness. Examples include:

I do like myself better each day
I do gain emotional strength each day
I do control my temper today
I do give others responsibility for their lives today
I do grow emotionally stronger each day
I do smile more today
I do praise my children today
I do feel good things about me today
I do sleep easily tonight
I do feel less guilt each day
I do face my fears courageously today
I do take on only what I can handle today
I do take care of me today
I do challenge myself to change today
I do manage my time better today
I do handle my finances wisely today
I do take a risk to grow today
I do choose to be happy today.

The daily use of these "I" statements is another form of self affirmation, designed to counter negative self-concept. It can result in a positive attitude, optimism, and can motivate you towards emotional growth and progress in your choice to choose happiness.

Another good way to focus on the positive in your life is to make up some affirmation cards and place them in places where you will see them often.

These forms of affirmation are words, phrases, or statements written on 3 x 5 index cards and placed where you can see them daily and be reminded of positive aspects about you. Every time you see these affirmation cards they will remind you to affirm yourself about these positive qualities or attributes. State all affirmations in a positive way.

Here are some places to put your affirmation cards:

mirror in bathroom	dashboard of car
mirror on dresser	desk at office
closet door	desk at home
refrigerator door	in your wallet
front door	in your brief case
bedroom door	in books you use at work
or school	
at your telephone	

Try some of these words to put on your affirmation cards: starting with "I am:"

bright	capable
creative	strong
intelligent	beautiful

smart	giving
quick	peaceful
loving	hopeful
caring	responsible
successful	problem solver
calm	quiet
pretty	handsome
relaxed	enjoyable

Consider some of these phrases as well: Just use "I" on these words.

- think happy
- am calm
- take action
- do it
- do it now
- am a winner
- take a risk
- dare to be different
- seize the blessing
- get in control
- let go
- let them be
- let it be
- health
- take it easy
- think wisely
- work smart
- take the time
- have fun
- relax and enjoy
- sit back
- step back
- take the lead
- give them space
- believe in me
- trust in me
- enjoy good

Affirmation statements can also be used to remind yourself that you are worthy and that you need to remain positive in all situations.

I can be a winner.
I am the best friend I have.
I have solved problems like this before.
I have the ability to handle this.
I am a capable human being.
I deserve to love and to be loved.
I am a skillful and artistic person.
I do show others a good example.
Letting go is best for them and for me.
They will thank me in the future.
Nothing is worth losing my sanity over.
I am responsible only for my own feelings.
I owe no one explanations for my behaviour, which is legally, morally, and ethically correct.
I deserve to have my rights recognized.

I am a deserving human being.
I deserve to enjoy the fruits of my labour.
I deserve to be rewarded for what I do.
I love myself for who I am.
It is OK to be selfish if I don't hurt anyone.
I like the way I handle problems.
I am able to handle any problem I face.
I have the right to feel the way I do.
My children will benefit from my healthy changes.
My children will survive my healthy changes.
My family will benefit from my relaxing more.
I deserve to relax more and take it easy.
There are beautiful things happening in my life daily.
I experience the excitement of growth daily.
Change is a blessing I am working toward.
Taking risks is the path to growth.
I grow in love daily.
I face each new day as a race to be won.

I am winning in the race of life.
I am a rich treasure ready to be found.
Let others know who I am.
Say hello to a new person today.
Open up to be loved today.
Be responsible. Relax!
Letting go is a loving act.
I am free of guilt today.
To be loved I must love.
God does not make junk.
There are opportunities in life to be tried.
My possibilities are endless.
Success is to be enjoyed.
Open myself up with one new person today.
Belief in self is a step toward personal growth.
I can handle all changes that come my way.
There is nothing I cannot handle.
Smile and let others in on the secret.

When you make a conscious effort to put these positive affirmations into your daily routine, you will be well on the way toward lifting your self-esteem and realizing your full potential as a meaningful and wonderful person! You will achieve your happiness within.

There are so many other steps you can do to raise your self-esteem and become everything you were meant to be. Let's move on!

Self-Nurturing

"I am only one, but still I am one. I cannot do everything, but still I can do something; and because I cannot do everything, I will not refuse to do something that I can do." Helen Keller

Rebutting your critical inner voice is an important step, but it is not enough. Since our self-esteem is in part due to how others have treated us in the past, the second step to more healthy self-esteem is to begin to treat yourself as a worthwhile person. Always remember "God Doesn't Make Junk."

Start to challenge past negative experiences or messages by nurturing and caring for yourself in ways that show that you are valuable, competent, deserving and lovable. There are several components to self-nurturing:

First and foremost, practice basic self-care. Get enough sleep, eat in a healthy fashion, get regular exercise, practice good hygiene, and so forth. A healthy mind is dependent on a healthy body. When you take care of the outside, it is natural that taking care of the inside will follow, which means more happiness within.

You should plan fun and relaxing things for yourself. You could go to a movie, take a nap, get a massage, plant a garden, get a new hairdo, or learn to meditate

- whatever you enjoy. Try new things to help you pamper yourself. For myself, I like reading a good book or just playing or doing something with my grandkids. Playing with the grandkids helps me be a kid again and we all need to remember to be a kid once in a while.

Reward yourself for your accomplishments – big and small! You could take the night off to celebrate good grades, spend time with a friend, or compliment yourself for making that hard phone call. It doesn't matter how small the accomplishment might seem, you deserve to celebrate every single little step. Try a little chocolate ice cream, or allow yourself to relax and just do nothing. It doesn't matter as long as it's a reward for YOU; whatever makes you happy!

You should always remind yourself of your strengths and achievements.

This may seem daunting – especially when you have a low self-image. How do you find those strengths?

One way is to make a list of things you like about yourself. Or keep a 'success' file of awards, certificates and positive letters or citations. Keep mementos of accomplishments you are proud of where you can see them. On anything and everything! No matter how small it may seem, if you succeeded and are proud of it, focus on it and celebrate!

A huge step you can take is to forgive yourself when you don't do all that you hoped to do. Self-nurturing can be surprisingly hard if you are not used to doing it. Don't be critical of yourself - remember that inner voice - when you don't do it just right. Reward yourself for trying in the first place. That's a huge step towards the positive YOU that you want to be! Remember you don't make mistakes, "they are learning experiences"!

There will be times when you don't feel you deserve to nurture yourself. This is when you need it the most! "Fake it" until you can "make it." When you treat yourself like you deserve to feel good and be nurtured, slowly you'll come to believe it. You'll be amazed at how you'll feel when you let go of the trash and embrace the jewels.

You may find yourself a bit lost during this process. It is also important to enlist the help of others in this process.

Calling Out "The Troops"

"Pick your friends out like you were choosing a fine piece of jewellery; they will always be there for you."
Debbie bills

Getting help from others is often the most important step a person can take to improve his or her self-esteem, but it can also be the most difficult. People with low self-esteem often don't ask for help because they feel they don't deserve it.

But since low self-esteem is often caused by how other people treated you in the past, you may need the help of other people in the present to challenge the critical messages that come from negative past experiences.

My husband has been a big help to me. You see at one time my self-esteem was low, but by understanding where the problem came from I have been able to fix it and find that happiness within.

Ask for support from your friends. Have them tell you what they like about you and what they think you do well. Have someone around just to vent your feelings to when you are feeling low. This person is your sounding board. He or she should allow you to express yourself without trying to fix things. This approach will make them happy to help and you happy to have someone listen to you. Even when we have good self esteem we do have low times. This is called, "being human."

You may also ask for a hug when you need one. Dr. Leo Buscaglia, also known as "The Hug Doctor", advocates hugging as a therapeutic measure in all situations. Sometimes the physical contact can fix anything by making you feel worthy of that hug. It may sound silly, but try it – it really does work!

Have you ever had a hard day and just need a hug? I know I have and so has my husband. Sometimes he'll come home and just say, "Can I have a hug?"

There are plenty of other people who can help you with your self-esteem. Talk to the people that love you and want to see you succeed. It makes people feel good to help, so don't take that away from them. We all need help of some sort in our lives.

When you don't ask for help, because you are afraid you will be bothering someone, you are making a decision for them. They have the right to make their own decisions. Don't let fear get in your way; people want to help.

Consider taking classes or trying out new activities to increase your sense of competence. You could take extra classes, join an exercise group, or find community classes in something that interests you such as scrap book keeping or karate. Get out of your comfort zone and choose to be happy one step at a time.

If the problem really is too overwhelming for you to deal with on your own, you may want to talk to a therapist or counsellor. Sometimes low self-esteem can feel so painful or difficult to overcome that the professional help of a therapist or counsellor is needed. Talking to a counsellor is a good way to learn more about your self-esteem issues and begin to improve your self-esteem. Just be sure you have a good counsellor. If you don't like what they say and it doesn't make sense, it is your inner voice telling you to try a new counsellor.

Positive Self-Talk

"Trust thy self; every heart vibrates to that iron string."
Bu Ralph Waldo Emerson

A critical first step is to realize and accept that you are not alone in this. Many, many people suffer from low self-esteem. They range from high-ranking government officials to celebrities to the postman or the lady down the road. They are all in this with you, whether they make it publicly known or not.

You need to realize that you are a wonderful, individual and special person - and there is no one quite like you. Your fingerprints and your DNA are totally different from everybody else's - unless you happen to have an identical twin.

And your mind - and how it thinks and operates - is absolutely your own. This means that out of six billion people in the world, you are a one-of-a-kind. So if nature has bothered to make you utterly unique, don't you feel that you should accept that you're important, and that you have as much right as anyone else to be to be happy?

You have other rights too. One of them is the right to make mistakes. Don't forget that 'to err is human', and most of us do much of our learning through getting things wrong before we get them right. Mistakes are learning experiences!

Furthermore, we have the right to respect ourselves - and to be respected: this is very important. And finally - and perhaps most vital of all - we have the right to say 'yes' or 'no' for ourselves. This is imperative for happiness within.

Many people with poor self-esteem think that they're not very important and that their views carry no weight. Is this you? If so, try to stop these destructive thoughts; because if you go around believing them, you'll encourage other people to believe them too. People see you like you see yourself.

Instead, start thinking of yourself - with your individual DNA, fingerprints and mind - as someone who has rights and opinions and ideas that are just as valid as anyone else's. This will help you to improve your 'self-estimation'.

The key to positive self-esteem is to remember that you have control over your situation: When feeling glum about a character flaw, remind yourself that you can take action to change yourself and shape your future. An example of this is, I don't like my nose (I have a birth mark on it), and so I do other things like making my hair attractive to draw attention away from my nose. I choose to be happy about other parts that I feel look better.

This is a good time to start keeping a journal – if you haven't already. Keeping a journal can be an amazingly therapeutic tool in raising not only your self-esteem, but also discovering new and exciting things about yourself that you might not have known.

Begin with a big project. In your journal, list 25 good things about you. This may seem like a daunting task, but I'm willing to bet that you can come up with them if you really try. Any time a negative thought pops into your head, push it out and write down what you were going to write in the first place.

You need to take stock of your positive qualities and your strengths. You have them; just look inside yourself. Can you whip up a mean batch of brownies? That's something! Maybe you're a whiz at surfing the net. Not everyone is adept at that – write it down! Every little thing counts, so take note and be proud!

The next thing I want you to do is write in your journal 10 things you want to improve in yourself. Don't look at these as your shortcomings or weaknesses. They are simply things you need or want to change. Next to each entry, write a way that you can change that aspect of yourself.

For example, if you feel you're lazy, go ahead and write that down, but also write down ways you could be less lazy. Find something that will motivate you - perhaps a reward system. It works in the schools; it could work with you too!

Don't concentrate on this list too much. The idea here is to acknowledge that there are parts of you that you want to work on and then set about doing just that!

Finally, take a moment to dream in your journal. Find something, or several things, which you would like to do. Maybe you want to learn to scuba dive. Write it down and make an action plan. You'll need to find a place that teaches scuba diving, and then enroll in the class!

Maybe you want to know more about Greek mythology. Call a community college and see if they offer a class and then sign up for it. Maybe you could find the class online. Just look and then go for it!

Now that you have a base journal, you need to accentuate the positive aspects of your life. Find a moment at the end of each day and write down at least one good thing that you did that day. Write down something that happened that you're proud of.

Maybe you stood up to a co-worker who's been giving you trouble. Perhaps you befriended that new person in the office. There is nothing too small to write here. Everything counts. We're focusing on the positive things in your life. When you have them down in black and white (or red or blue – whatever ink colour you prefer) they become real and true. That's what you should focus on – every day!

You will also need to give yourself a little pep talk daily. Don't base your perception of yourself on what others think of you. This is destructive. No one else knows you better than you! Look in the mirror every morning and say something positive.

"My hair looks great"

"I can do anything I want to do"

"I am a worthy person and people should listen to me"

Etc.

It can be anything at all – as long as it's something positive about you. Remember that everyone feels this way sometimes. Don't compare yourself to others. Even the popular girl thinks nobody likes her. You are a unique individual with great qualities that you can share. Stand up and be heard!

Often we make ourselves unhappy because we go over and over mistakes that we have made. But we can feel happier, and improve our self-esteem, if we re-think those things we believe we have done wrong or badly.

When you have a bad day, or something goes wrong in your relationship or at work, write in your journal an account of what went right with that episode, not what went wrong. The results will surprise you - and improve how you see yourself. Your happiness within is going to improve.

The Secret to Happiness is Good Self-Esteem

"No one can make you feel inferior without your consent." Eleanor Roosevelt

Healthy self-esteem originates in the environment found in the family, school, peer group, work place, and community. There are certain characteristics of your environment that need to be personally present in order for self-esteem to be fostered and grow. This will certainly help with your happiness within.

The main component of a healthy environment is that it needs to be nurturing. It should definitely provide unconditional warmth, love, and caring. It needs to provide the realization that other people are recognized as deserving to be nurtured, reinforced, rewarded, and bonded to.

The environment transmits messages of warmth, loving, and caring by physically touching, meeting the survival needs of food, clothing and shelter, and providing a sense of stability and order in life.

A healthy environment should provide acceptance, which bring happiness within. It will recognize that other people see each other as worthy individuals who have a unique set of personality characteristics, skills, abilities, and competencies, making them special.

Acceptance helps individuals recognize that differences among and between people are OK, and this encourages the development of a sense of personal mastery and autonomy. Acceptance enables people to develop relationships with others, yet maintain healthy boundaries of individuality within themselves.

There should be good communication. Everyone should be heard and responded to in a healthy way so that healthy problem solving is possible. Appropriate giving and receiving of feedback is encouraged and rewarded. Communicating at a "feelings" level is a mode of operation for these people, allowing them to be in touch with their emotions in a productive manner.

For the environment to support the development of healthy self-esteem it must contain recognition and acceptance of people for who they are. That recognition and acceptance should not be based on the condition that they must first conform to a prescribed standard of behaviour or conduct. This is unhealthy. Unconditional recognition and acceptance given in the form of support allows individuals to reach their ultimate potential and enjoy being happy.

There should be clearly defined and enforced limits known to individuals with no hidden tricks or manipulation. Limits set the structure for the lives of individuals, allowing clear benchmarks of appropriate and inappropriate behaviour. Limits enable individuals to recognize their responsibilities and to chart their course of behaviour in a rational way.

Respect and latitude for individual action within the defined limits of the environment should be present as well. This encourages individuals to use their creativity, ingenuity, and imagination to be productive within the established structure. Restrictions that suppress individuality can lead to a narrow focus, with people becoming stunted and handicapped in the use of their personal skills, abilities, and resources.

There should also be established freedom within the structure. This enables individuals to develop a sense of personal autonomy. If they are too tied down and inhibited they could become resentful and eventually rebellious against the prescribed structures in their environment.

Being given the freedom of self-expression within the established rules and norms allows individuals to explore their potential to its fullest; thus there is a greater possibility of becoming successful, healthy achievers and obviously living a life of happiness within.

Finally, there should be bonding, which is the physical/emotional phenomenon between individuals and the others in their environment. This is necessary for the development of healthy self-esteem.

Bonding is forming a mutual emotional attachment between an individual and a "significant other" (parent, child, friend, lover, etc.). This involves the significant other giving unconditional love and support as well as developing an emotional link between each other.

Bonding provides a sense of emotional security and stability. It allows you to be free to explore all that is wonderful about you and the people around you without fear of reproach or ridicule. This will develop a healthy self-image and sense of identity. Bonding also will give all involved a sense of belonging and mattering in the "big picture".

Bonding can be achieved in many ways. You allow the other person to enter a strange environment while providing support and "cheer leading" the entire way. It encourages the other person to be self-confident and offers up help with individual problems while being encouraging that any problem can be overcome.

If you want to bond effectively with those around you, there are some things you can do.

Talk face to face with people

- Use physical touch when interacting
- Work at meeting the "match" of the person by encouraging him to do things for which he is ready and capable
- Speak in a loving, caring manner
- Show respect
- Listen carefully; offer empathy and understanding
- Be honest when describing or dealing with problems
- Be supportive as they face the harsh realities of life and become fearful, scared, or concerned about the future

- Let the person grow to be his own person by encouraging the development of independent and autonomous thinking
- Assist in becoming a good problem solver by encouraging open exploration and discussion of options and alternatives when facing problems at home, school, work, or in the community.

If you feel you aren't bonding with the people around you, show them this list. Ask them to help you on your journey towards healthy self-esteem. Our guess is they'll be happy to help! When given a choice we always want to choose happiness.

In general, you need to make the environment conducive to the positive aspects of you and your inner voice. Surround yourself with people who are loving, caring, and supportive. Stay away from those people who are fountains of negativity. They'll only bring you down. They love to take away your happiness within.

Look at your surroundings. At work, do you have a work space that fosters positive emotions? Place pictures of your loved ones around you. Add a pretty flowering plant. Post motivational sayings where you can always see them.

You should have happiness within at your own home and be happy to arrive there at the end of the day. Personalize your house, hang pictures you love, drawings from kids, motivational quotes, posters, arts and crafts. Use anything that makes you feel good. So what if you don't have perfect décor. Make yourself happy and serene. Surround yourself with what <u>you</u> think of as beauty.

If you are in a negative environment, the logical answer is to change it. But what if you can't? Not everyone can just up and quit a job that is an unhealthy environment. The thing is that it isn't always easy to change that which is negative.

There are, however, things you can do to minimize the negativity. There are certain people and situations that will threaten your self-esteem. You need to stay away from these in order to maintain the happiness and positive thinking you are trying hard to cultivate.

At work, beware of the "dog eat dog" theory where everyone else is fighting just to get ahead. This is where non-appreciative people usually thrive. No one will be grateful for your contributions even if you miss lunch and dinner, and stay up late. Most of the time you work too much without getting help from the people concerned. Stay out of this; it will ruin your self esteem. Competition is at stake anywhere. Be healthy enough to compete, but in a healthy competition.

With people: Bulldozers, brown nosing, gossipmongers, whiners, backstabbers, snipers, the walking wounded, controllers, naggers, complainers, exploders, all these kinds of people will pose bad vibes for your self esteem, as well as jeopardise your self improvement scheme.

Change: Change challenges our paradigms. It tests our flexibility, adaptability and alters the way we think. Change will make life difficult for a while, it may cause stress but it will help us find ways to improve our selves. Change will be there forever, we must be susceptible to it. Focus on the positive parts of the change. It will take some getting used to, but remember the old adage "change is good."

Past Experiences: It's okay to cry and say "ouch!" when we experience pain. But don't let pain transform itself into fear. It might grab you by the tail and swing you around. Treat each failure and mistake as a lesson. Acknowledge it, get past it, and don't dwell on it. Letting go of the past is so important in a healthy lifestyle. We can't change what has happened to us in the past. It's important to focus on the future.

The World: There are so many awful things that happen in this world. It can bring most people down. Don't wrap yourself up with all the negativities of the world. In building self esteem, we must learn how to make the best out of bad situations.

Genetics: The way you are and your behavioural traits is said to be a mixed end product of your inherited traits (genetics), your upbringing (psychic), and your environmental surroundings such as your spouse, the company, the economy or your circle of friends. You have your own identity. If your father is a failure, it doesn't mean you have to be a failure too. Learn from other people's experience, so you'll never have to encounter the same mistakes.

Remember to keep yourself in a positive environment as much as possible. Don't let others put their trash in your mind. You wouldn't let them put trash in your house. Clearly be yourself and do what makes you happy.

Kids and Self-Esteem

"Children are a creation in the works. Never underestimate them and always pay attention to their talents. If they cannot run fast teach them to hit the ball out of the park." Debbie Bills

None of us were born with low self-worth or low self-esteem. It developed through the years by what we were told and how we were made to feel by the people in our lives. Whether you have children or not, you can make a difference in a child's view of how they see themselves and stop the cycle of low self-esteem problems, which is certainly going to help make a happy adult.

Obviously first step toward fostering a good self-image in children is to provide them with unconditional love and caring. Don't criticize or berate them. Always focus on the positives and provide encouragement in everything they do.

More specifically, however, there are many, many other things you can do. First, you should model good self-esteem. Express through your actions and words that you respect yourself. Children are wonderful at imitating what they see and hear. Be a good role model. If you have happiness within as a parent it will clearly show to a child.

Create positive routines. Young children need routines to help them to feel secure and competent.

Try to set a good schedule for bedtime, rest/naps, meals, etc. Try to keep exceptions to the routine to a minimum and explain any necessary changes if/when they occur. This is slowly going to start them on their way to happiness within.

Allow many opportunities for children to contribute to the family. Give the child a job/chore that only he/she does for the family. Even a small job can have a positive lasting impact on a child's self esteem. Always let the child know how happy you are with the job well done.

Talk about the world in positive terms. Even though there is negativity in the world, don't dwell on it with a child. Be sure to point out the many positive things in the world to children.

Give them the gift of your time. Remember quality is more important than quantity. Even if you spend just 30 minutes with a child one on one - playing games, taking walks, having long bedtime chats, or just snuggling in front of the TV, spending time with a child shows them that you value their company and this is extremely important for their happiness within.

Give them choices. By giving children choices between a reasonable set of options that are already predetermined, you will make them feel empowered. But be cautious here. It is definitely clear that at times you cannot give them a choice. You don't want to endanger them in any way, but point out the dangers. Too much control sends the message that your children can't adequately handle their lives. Too little control sends the message that you don't care, so you must strike a balance between these two extremes and give them more freedom as they grow older.

Acknowledge and listen to their thoughts and emotions since they are so much a part of who they are. Listening with empathy says you care about what they think and feel. Plus it will create an atmosphere in which they will be more willing to listen to you. Show them the positive side of their choices and the negative side if there is one. In this way their confidence will grow in the ability to make right choices, which bring happiness.

You don't always have to agree with your kids when you listen to them, nor let them do whatever they want. You can have a different view on a situation and still understand their perspective. And you may still have to discipline them even if you better understand why they misbehaved. It is especially important to always explain why they are being disciplined.

You should structure situations so your children experience more success than failure. Don't expect standards of performance which they cannot achieve. You want them to grow up with far more praise than criticism, more accomplishments than failures. It is extremely important to teach them that a failure is just a learning experience to help them grow into a happy adult.

Let your children know they are lovable and capable. Again, this is a self-evident principle. You should give your children daily expressions of affection - hugs, kisses, words of love, praise and appreciation. Think of them as cups of love which you want to fill with as much caring as you can. When we know that we are lovable happiness within comes into play.

Provide security for them. Children need to feel secure. Few feel secure when there are conflicts occurring around them. Few can relax inwardly when others around them are shouting, accusing, criticizing and hating each other. To a small child, tension between parents, or between parents and the child or other children, constitute a deep chasm of insecurity. Plus, they may end up blaming themselves for the conflicts around them.

Avoid arguing around them as much as possible. If they do see conflict, make sure they also see resolution of the conflict. Not everything in life is peaches and cream and problems do arise. People will argue – it's a fact of life. The important part here is that the child sees a peaceful resolution in the end. This will teach them problem solving skills and help them realize that even though there is conflict in the world, there is also a way to resolve it in ways that everyone benefits from.

Our children need to know that we accept and love them regardless of what they may do, but also that certain forms of behaviour are not acceptable to us. Let them know that you love them, but it is obviously the behaviour that isn't acceptable.

We must be very clear about why we are rejecting certain behaviour. Our rejection can come out of a place of real love and concern for the child, if, in fact, we are not simply protecting our own interests. As long as certain behaviour does no real harm to anyone, it is best to allow the child to pursue it. Something within them, some need is guiding them to explore that kind of activity. They have something to learn through doing that. Learning and obviously making their own decisions sometimes helps them choose happiness, even if it is not the right choice. This gives them a chance to learn by their mistakes.

This does not mean that there are not moments where control or even natural or logical consequences may be necessary. But we need to be sure that the reasons are valid and have to do with real issues of safety or morality and not because we are disappointed with their grades or selection of hobbies, interests or friends.

In order to love our children unconditionally, we will need to start loving ourselves unconditionally. We will have to let go of all the prerequisites we have put on our own self-love. We will need to love ourselves even though we are not perfect, even though we make mistakes, even when others do not love and accept us. The more we free our self-love from the various prerequisites, the more our love for our children and others will become unconditional. In return you are going to find greater happiness within for yourself.

Finally, we must provide positive reinforcement for our children. Everyone likes a pat on the back, recognition, strokes, praise or affirmation of his or her ability, goodness and worthiness. Our children have not yet formed images of which they are and need these positive inputs even more than adults. Children are not sure if they are able or not. They are small in such a large world. They are learning and thus making many mistakes as they try to learn how to do things correctly.

In our attempt to help our children we often tend to point out their mistakes more frequently than their successes. The mistakes are what are more obvious and thus we feel the need to point them out. The successes are taken for granted. We over-emphasize what our children do wrong. This undermines their sense of ability, and they start to doubt whether they can really succeed.

Thus they become preoccupied, worrying about whether they will be able to do it, and whether they will be criticized. Thus little energy is left for focusing on what they are actually doing so that they can do it correctly and succeed. Then, if our children's performance suffers, we become even more critical. This creates a vicious circle in which our children's sense of ability, success and worthiness is completely undermined.

So, the easy thing to say is just "Don't do this". If you find yourself overly criticizing a child or yelling berating comments at them, take a moment, count to 10 and think of a healthier way to address the situation. They will be better for it – and so will you!

What about that huge area that is especially difficult to deal with? It's bound to happen, but don't let it swallow you! Criticism can be given and accepted graciously without affecting your self-esteem. This can be shown to them when you have made a mistake and you let them know that you were wrong.

Coping With Criticism

"He has a right to criticize, who has a heart to help."
Abraham Lincoln

One of the areas that people with low self-esteem have greatest difficulty with is criticism - giving as well as receiving it. Both can be extraordinarily difficult. In fact some individuals are absolutely demolished by criticism, but it's something we cannot avoid. If we honestly want to find happiness within, learning to deal with criticism is a must.

Now, criticism is often unfair and when it is we need to counter it by putting our own case clearly and calmly. But some criticism is justified - and when we're sensible we can learn from it. An example of this is; I have a habit of interrupting my husband when we are talking. He has very nicely brought this to my attention. It does annoy him very much and I have chosen to learn from this and work hard at correcting this habit. It is my choice, because it takes away from his happiness and my happiness within when I annoy him.

Often when we're criticized, we're so hurt that we start excusing ourselves and rebutting what's being said without really listening to it.

A mature, self-possessed person listens to criticism without interrupting. If there are aspects to the criticism that are valid, just begin by agreeing with those points. If you're unsure of what's being said, ask for clarification. If indeed you are wrong, say so and apologize. But if you disagree with the criticism, smile and say: 'I'm afraid I don't agree with you.' "It seems we definitely have a different opinion about this."

Now, it takes quite a lot of practice to feel and act this cool. So let's go through it again. When someone criticizes you: listen - don't interrupt or start excusing yourself

- agree - where possible
- ask for clarification
- when you're wrong, admit it and apologize
- if criticism is wrong or unfair say: 'I'm afraid that I don't agree with you'

Now, let's look at giving criticism, because people with poor-self esteem often find it harder to dish out criticism than receive it. In fact many adults actually avoid promotion because they can't face the prospect of being in authority and having to criticize others.

So, how can you learn to criticize when you have to?

First of all, keep calm. Second, try to make your criticism at an appropriate time, rather than waiting till you're so fed up that you're furiously angry - when you'll be bound to make a mess of it.

Take some deep breaths when you know you've got to criticize someone. Then try a technique called the 'criticism sandwich'. This means that you say something nice to the person you're criticizing, then you insert the criticism, then you end with something else that's nice or positive or flattering.

Let me give you an example using my habit of interrupting my husband. He says; "Honey I love you a lot, but I go nuts when you interrupt me when we are talking." "Thank you, I feel better being allowed to say that, it is appreciated."

You might notice that people who are good and fair when they criticize, tend to use the word 'I' rather than the word 'you'. This is because the word 'I' shows you're in control and that you've thought about what you're saying.

All too frequently when we're out of control we don't say anything initially, which is when we should address the problem. Instead we bottle it up till we explode. Then we use the words 'you', 'you're' and 'your' all the time. We say: 'You're lazy.' Or 'You make me sick.'

These kinds of phrases sound very angry and accusatory. They also show that we're not in control. And after uttering them we generally feel worse about ourselves and our self-esteem plummets even more.

So just to recap, when criticizing:

- use the word 'I', not the word 'you'
- keep calm and do some deep breathing

- use the 'criticism sandwich' technique

- always try to criticize a person's behaviour rather than the person

These tips are just as handy when it comes to standing up for yourself in other situations. And they're very useful when you want to be able to say 'no' without feeling guilty. Just keep calm and use the word 'I'.

Say: 'I won't be coming to that party with you.' Or; 'I can't work late tonight, I'm sorry. But if necessary I'll happily stay tomorrow.' And never, ever apologize for saying no. It's your right – exercise it.

People with poor self-esteem are always getting talked into doing things that they don't want to do. Does this sound like you? If so, it must stop if you want to value yourself more. So learning how to stay calm and just say 'no' is very important.

Now that we've looked at different ways you can combat low self-esteem, the next section is a quick start guide. It's packed with tips on how to start raising your self-esteem – right now!

I think you are going to really enjoy this. It does not take a life time to rebuild your self-esteem. Trust me, I have been there. My mother had low self-esteem and she didn't even realize she was producing it with her children. She just thought she was teaching us and protecting her children.

That is why I cannot stress good self-esteem enough. If you don't have it get it, so your child doesn't have to pay the price for not having good self-esteem. They will love you deeply for that gift. It will instill happiness within for them their whole life.

Conclusion

"Common looking people are the best in the world; that is the reason the Lord made so many of them."
Abraham Lincoln

Your self-esteem is like a star at night that shines brightest when it is the darkest. It is your inner light that burns brightly and freely no matter what is happening around you. A Zen saying reminds us: "What was your original face before you were born?"

Have you ever just watched a one or two year old? They don't care, they are just busy doing what they like. It is really refreshing. Even if you are in a store or restaurant and there is a child there either being cute or kicking up a storm, they're just doing their thing and it doesn't really matter who is around. They haven't learned about self-esteem, yet. Nothing is holding them back from being who they really are. They have happiness within.

Self-esteem is perfectly intact when we are born, in fact, it is inherent in us; however, it often diminishes over the course of our childhood. We lose a little of it whenever we fail, make mistakes, misbehave, feel guilty, refuse to forgive, neglect ourselves, and/or do things we are ashamed of. As an adult, we sometimes feel as if our "self" is in pieces - that we are somehow not whole and complete.

This is not true. We are whole and complete even with our missing pieces and broken parts. We just need to decide to gather ourselves up and become whole again. I am willing to bet that when you look back over your life, the first thing that comes to mind is the regrets, the sad times in your past.

Do you see the pieces of yourself lying along the path of your life? The ones where you didn't feel good enough, or where you were criticized or blamed by someone else? But have you ever stopped to look at the memories of when you won the prize, felt really great, on top of the world - those moments that prove what a wonderfully amazing human being you are?

It is your birthright to love and honour yourself. The good news is that you can reclaim that which is yours. That is your self-esteem.

There is absolutely no reason at all why people should "suffer" from low self esteem. Your self esteem is something over which you have absolute and immediate control. Think of self esteem as a muscle; it never stays the same for any period of time.

Like any muscle it either weakens or gets stronger. Self esteem improvement is like exercising a muscle. It relies on small incremental improvement on a daily basis. You won't run out to the gym and have perfect muscles for life in an hour. Consistent self esteem improvement is the only way to lasting success and an increase in the quality of your life every day you live it.

Your self-esteem contributes to your vitality, energy level, persistence, happiness within and personal magnetism. Self-esteem is about what is on the inside; a belief in yourself and your abilities. Positive esteem focuses on acceptance of self and others. It remains constant despite the storm. This fosters cooperation and wholeness.

Building self esteem will eventually lead to self improvement if we start to become responsible for who we are, what we have and what we do. It's like a flame that should gradually spread like a brush fire from inside and out. When we develop self esteem, we take control of our mission, values and discipline. Self esteem brings about self improvement, true assessment, and determination.

Be positive. Be contented and happy. Be appreciative. Never miss an opportunity to compliment. A positive way of living will help you build self esteem, your starter guide to self improvement.

"Don't hold yourself back by who you think you aren't." Debbie Bills

It is never too late to build your self-esteem. You can start RIGHT NOW! Self-esteem has a big impact on how we enjoy life. Respect others, yourself, and life in general. Practice the techniques we have given you every single day. Watch them work wonders in your life.

Take Command of Your Self-Esteem

Become the person you can be and treat yourself well. You deserve it! Take out that piece of paper and write down all your good points and concentrate on them. Write down your talents (everyone has them) and use them to their fullest. You have something to add to this world and this world needs you. Find your good self-esteem and you will find your happiness within. Remember; it is your birth right.

Remember; God doesn't make junk, which makes you very special, and there is no one with your DNA.

Debbie Bills

Debbie Bills has built her personal Happy Maker website over the last 2 years. She now provides the tips and ideas for living a life of complete happiness within.

This is what she says about herself:

The older that I got the more I was beginning to realize my life just wasn't on track. Having been raise by an alcoholic father and a mother with very low self-esteem I knew I had my work cut out for me.

I was just making all the wrong decision in life. Being newly divorced with 3 daughters to raise I needed to get to the bottom of who I really was. After much research, reading and evaluating I found my answers and knew that I was a survivor. I no longer had to withdraw from the world, but could be a part of it.

Through her life trials and tribulations Debbie has learned from the inside out what the true meaning of living a happy life means.

Check out all her tips, ideas and living experience at:
http://www.happymakernow.com/blog/

www.ingramcontent.com/pod-product-compliance
Ingram Content Group UK Ltd.
Pitfield, Milton Keynes, MK11 3LW, UK
UKHW041413180426
11947UKWH00007B/101